Max makes breakfast

It was Grandad's birthday.
Kerry was wrapping up the present she had bought.
'All I have to do now is find him a really
    special birthday card,' she thought.
Then she had a better idea.

'I know. I'll *make* him a card,' she thought.
  'I'll paint a picture of Max and me on the front.
  He'll like that.'
She got her paints and a holiday photograph
  of her and Max.

2

It was Saturday and it was still very early.
Mum and Dad were not up yet.
Kerry decided to do her painting on the kitchen
  table.

It wasn't easy to do the painting.

The colours kept running into each other, and she
didn't have the right sort of green for Max's
swimming trunks.

'I'll just have to paint them blue,' she thought.

It was a long time before Kerry's painting began
  to look right.
She still had a lot of work to do on it when Dad
  came downstairs.
'Oh no!' he groaned. 'Is that the time?'

'You'll have to move all your things off the table,
  Kerry,' said Dad. 'I've got to make Max's
  breakfast before Mum and I go shopping.'
'But I can't!' said Kerry. 'I'm just getting
  to the difficult bit.'

Dad came to see what Kerry was doing.
'I see,' he said. 'It's two monkeys in the zoo.'
'Dad!' said Kerry. 'It's a painting of Max and me.'
'I was talking about the photograph,' laughed Dad.

'I'll do a deal with you,' said Dad. 'You don't have
to clear the table if you'll dress Max and give
him his breakfast when he wakes up. Mum and I
want to get to the supermarket before it gets
crowded. But be quiet. Grandad is still asleep.'
'It's a deal,' said Kerry.

8

Dad and Mum had only been gone for a few minutes
   when Max came downstairs.

'Bubbles hungry. Max hungry,' said Max.

Bubbles was Max's teddy.

'I shan't be long,' said Kerry. 'Nearly finished!'

Max went to the fridge and opened the door.
Max began to take things out of the fridge and
   mix them together on the floor.
Kerry wasn't watching him.
She was too interested in Grandad's birthday card.

It was quite a while before Kerry noticed what
  Max was doing.
'Max!' she yelled. 'Stop it at once!'
'Bubbles breakfast,' smiled Max. 'Bubbles hungry.'

Kerry stopped painting and cleared up the mess.
'You're a very naughty boy,' she said. 'Go upstairs
and play with Bubbles. When you come down
again I'll have finished my painting. Then I'll
make your breakfast.'
Max and Bubbles went upstairs.

Max tried to dress himself but he wasn't good at it.
He kept putting his arms in the wrong sleeves and
 his feet in the wrong legs.
Everything seemed to be back to front.

Max went into Mum and Dad's room to look at
  himself in the mirror.
There were all sorts of exciting things on Mum's
  dressing table.
This gave Max an idea.

He decided to make another breakfast for Bubbles.
First he got some white powder and poured it
   on to a pillow.
Then he found some cream and added that.
Then he poured perfume into the mixture.

When Max had finished making breakfast for
  Bubbles he sat his teddy on the bed.
Max couldn't find a spoon so he had to use a comb.
'Breakfast Bubbles,' he said. 'Eat breakfast.'

Bubbles didn't seem to like his breakfast.
He wouldn't open his mouth properly.
'Bad Bubbles!' said Max crossly. 'Eat breakfast.'
Bubbles was soon covered in a sticky mess.

17

Downstairs, Kerry had finished her painting.

She was just writing the words.

She had got as far as Happy Birt when she stopped
and looked up.

'That's funny,' she thought. 'Max is very quiet.'

Kerry was worried.

'He's either being very good, or very bad,'
   she thought.

She went upstairs to look for Max.

She could smell perfume.

Kerry went into Mum and Dad's bedroom.

'Max!' she gasped. 'What on earth have you been
   doing? Just look at the mess! What's Mum going
   to say?'

'Max make breakfast,' said Max.

'You've wasted all Mum's best perfume,' wailed
   Kerry, and she burst into tears.
When Kerry began to cry, Max began to cry too.
'How ever are we going to clear up all the mess?'
   sobbed Kerry.

Just then, Grandad came into the bedroom.
'What ever is the matter?' he asked kindly.
Kerry told him the whole story.
Grandad looked thoughtful.

'Now, now,' said Grandad. 'It's my birthday
    today. Everybody is supposed to be happy.
    I'll tell you what we'll do,' said Grandad to Kerry.
    'First of all you must get Max and Bubbles
    cleaned up, while I sort out the
    mess in the bedroom.'

Kerry took Max to the bathroom and washed and
  dressed him properly.
Then she got lots of soapy water and washed the
  mess off Bubbles.
'Bubbles covered in bubbles,' said Max.

Grandad sorted out the mess in the bedroom and put
   the bedclothes in the washing machine.
'There now,' he said. 'Things don't look so bad.'
'Bubbles hungry,' said Max.

Grandad made breakfast for himself and Max.

'Mum and Dad will never know about the mess,' said
  Grandad.

'But what about Mum's perfume?' asked Kerry.

  'It's all gone.'

'We'll buy some more,' said Grandad.

'But Mum and Dad will be home soon,' wailed Kerry.

'We'll have to be quick,' said Grandad.

'With any luck it will take them ages to finish the shopping. We'll have to do the best we can.'

When they had finished their breakfast Grandad took
Kerry, Max and Bubbles to the chemist.
Grandad bought some more perfume for Mum, and
all the other things that Max had used.

As they came out of the shop Kerry saw Mum and Dad.
They were talking to Mrs Thomas.
'We'll have to be quick,' said Grandad. 'We've just
    got time to get home before them.'

Grandad, Kerry and Max were first home.
Grandad put clean bedclothes on the bed.
Kerry put the things they had bought on Mum's
   dressing table.
'Just in time!' said Grandad.

'Hello, everyone,' said Mum. 'I hope Kerry and Max
   haven't been any bother, Grandad?'
'Of course not,' smiled Grandad. 'They've been as
   quiet as mice and as good as gold.'
'That makes a change,' laughed Dad.

Everybody gave Grandad his presents.
'Thank you for the lovely card, Kerry,'
   said Grandad. 'Did you make it yourself?'
'Yes,' said Kerry. 'It took me most of the morning.'
'Very nice,' said Mum. 'But why does it say
   Happy Birt?'